The PRIORITY MANAGER

TURNING YOUR INTENTIONS INTO ACTIONS

OVERCOMING BARRIERS
TO PERSONAL SUCCESS

BY DANIEL STAMP

D0800145

Copyright © 1993 Kronos Learning Inc.

ISBN # 0-9697420-0-2

All rights reserved.

No part of this book may be reproduced in any form
by any means without the written permission of the publisher,
except by a reviewer who may quote passages in a review.

PRODUCTION

Cover Design and Illustration: Suburbia Studios, Victoria, Canada
Typesetting: Sunray Graphics, Vancouver, Canada
Photography: Back cover photo by Kent Kallberg Studios, Vancouver, Canada
Printing: Darwin Industries, Vancouver, Canada

PUBLISHED BY

Priority Management Systems Inc.
International Headquarters: IBM Tower, P.O. Box 10105
1700-701 West Georgia Street
Vancouver, B.C.
Canada V7Y 1C6

Printed and bound in Canada

T A B L E O F C O N T E N T S

MY PERSONAL ODYSSEY

*Every now and again
a door opens and
lets the future in.*

GRAHAM GREENE

THERE ARE SIXTEEN PINK SLIPS SCATTERED

in front of you, all marked urgent. The telephone has taken on a life of its own, every line buzzing and flashing. Scrolls of faxes and computer print-outs cascade off your desk and onto the floor. The new product launch begins in three minutes. Today is your son's birthday and you realize you're not sure how old he is. Your daughter's softball league final is this afternoon and she wants you to come. You've been asked to entertain an out-of-town client after work. Your diary has been sucked into the black hole of your desk – it could be under any number of project file folders. For a brief, dizzying moment, you can't even remember what day of the week it is.

It's time for a test.

Take a moment and close your eyes. This could be the most important test you've ever taken. I call it The Tombstone Test.

If tomorrow was going to be your last day, what would you see written on your tombstone? He never left the office before 6 o'clock? She faithfully ate lunch at her desk everyday? Or would it be something relating to your life? Imagine your family gathered around – what would they see written there? He was a great father; she was a great sister; he/she was a great friend; <u>or</u>; the first quarter results were good?

Only you can determine your epitaph. And if what you imagine written there today is frighteningly out of synch with how you'd like to be remembered, it's high time to take control of your future.

I should know. Several years ago, I failed my own Tombstone Test.

I had come into the North American business world after working in academia overseas. I was a science educator in the U.K. and Africa and a professor at the University of the South Pacific in Fiji.

The academic life had allowed me more time with my wife and three daughters than when I began my own business in 1980. One day in late 1983, I realized that because I had been so single-mindedly pursuing my business goals, I wasn't fulfilling my emotional role with the family. My children were rapidly changing and growing up, and I wasn't really around to witness it. My determination to succeed in the business world was robbing me of time with my daughters, time I would never get back. There was a personal gap in my life that my work obsession couldn't fill.

The overwhelming irony was that at that same time I was on the threshold of expanding my time management company. In tandem with my desire to get to know my family again, it dawned on me that time management alone wasn't enough. Up until then I had been rather proud of my aptitude for managing time. But somewhere along the way – while stuffing as many activities into a 24-hour day as possible – I'd lost track of my priorities and personal goals. I wasn't managing my life, I was merely managing to meet my deadlines.

It was out of that experience that I developed the principles of Priority Management™, a values-based way of time-management and decision-making. In 1984 I started Priority Management in Vancouver, British Columbia. Today, Priority Management spans the globe, having grown into an international network of over 350 independently-owned and operated offices. From Vancouver, B.C. to Atlanta, Georgia, and London, England to Sydney, Australia, Priority Management's associates have successfully trained more than half a million clients to return to values-based time management and turn their intentions into actions.

Our results have been astounding. Consider some of these statistics: A 41% increase in the ability to manage projects. A 26% decrease in interruptions. A 61% increase in the ability to effectively delegate. Productive time increased by more than an hour a day. And, most important of all, a great majority of clients report a more balanced lifestyle – a full 80% now include personal, social and family activities along with business commitments in their daily plans.

The ability to manage priorities is considered by many to be the most vital skill in the new Information Age Economy. In today's Information Age, or New Knowledge Economy (the focus of the next chapter), interdependence is one of the keys to productivity. Our worldwide network consists of a group of independent, self-motivated individuals who have realized just how much they can achieve by working together. Priority Management's associates are the vanguard of the Knowledge Age. Having mastered the essential management skills needed to thrive in the new economy and lead a balanced personal/business life, they are now passing these on to others.

I believe one of the great challenges of the New Knowledge Economy will be to increase the productivity of 'white collar' work. The answer lies in identifying and measuring the processes and competencies of knowledge work. Priority Management has identified these processes of knowledge work and has developed a way of measuring competencies for individuals. But first, we have to master the tools of knowledge work. And you already have one of the most effective productivity tools of all –The Priority Manager personal organizer system.

I find that a lot of people think someone is born with these competencies – that biology is destiny and essential management skills are somehow genetically carried. That couldn't be farther from the truth. As someone with a lot of experience in the adult education field, I'm convinced these management skills are learned, not inherent.

You, too, can become a Priority Manager. This book expands on the concepts of Priority Management training and serves as a resource you can return to for a quick "refresher". It will show you how to discover the power of your potential through increased productivity, reduced stress and a more balanced, higher quality life. And it will demonstrate that being a Priority Manager means doing the right things, not just doing things right. You've already taken that first step by attending Priority Management training. Keep your Priority Manager system at hand while you are reading this so you can capture ideas that will help you turn your intentions into actions.

When I reflect on the Odyssey I've undertaken to become a Priority Manager, I'm reminded at times of Ulysses, that unhappy wanderer of ancient lore. By the poet Homer's account, after the Trojan War, Ulysses spent ten long years on his Odyssey back to Ithaca and his wife and son. Thousands of years later the story of Ulysses still fascinates us, I think, because he was a man who mastered his destiny and finally made it home after overcoming many obstacles. Maybe that's what we're all trying to do in a sense – make it home. Whether literally – becoming a 5 o'clock mom or dad again – or metaphorically – to yourself and your values, "making it home" means taking control of our lives in an ever-changing world.

You can look upon your journey to be a Priority Manager as a personal Odyssey. Whether you're Ulysses battling one-eyed giants and weathering storms at sea, or a manager negotiating your way through a mind-numbing series of conflicting commitments, it's well worth the trip once you've arrived "home".

Once again, I should know. My son was born in 1985, two years after I realized the value of managing my priorities, and we've both been rewarded as a result. I've been with him every step of the way, and he knows his dad. My wife and daughters are happier now, too. They've got a friend and companion in me, not just a breadwinner.

I run an international business. Conceivably, I could sit at my desk 24 hours a day, because there is never a minute of that 24 hours that we don't have an office open somewhere. But I go home at 5:30. I hope your experience with Priority Management helps you get "home". Happy Odyssey!

Daniel Stamp
Vancouver, 1993

THE INFORMATION BIG BANG

Nothing endures
but change.

HERACLITUS, 540 B.C.

THE BIG BANG, LEADING SCIENTIFIC
theorists say, brought the universe – including Earth – into being. Some 4700 million years later, the Earth is being subjected to another cataclysmic explosion, one that has shaken the very foundations of how we live our lives. This second Big Bang occurred in the last half of the 20th century and involved an information explosion from which people are still reeling.

Information bombards us daily, multiplying with rabbit-like intensity. Consider this: experts say that information now *doubles* every two years; paperwork has increased 600 percent in the last two decades and North American business generates one billion documents every day. A weekday issue of The New York Times contains more information than the average person in the 16th century would encounter in an entire lifetime.

Even the cycle of innovation and production has telescoped inwards at a dizzying rate. It took 112 years from the development of the early daguerreotype for photography to become a commercial enterprise. That cycle then shrank to a mere 56 years between Alexander Graham Bell's invention of the telephone and its commercial use. Television went into commercial production 12 years after its invention. At the beginning of this decade, IBM's product development cycle was three years from invention to production. Competition has rapidly forced the high-tech giant to cut its product cycle time down to as little as six months.

At the time of the Information Big Bang, we moved irrevocably from an economy of mass production to one of mass information – head-on into the future. Manufacturing jobs are rapidly disappearing, radically transforming the economic landscape. Today, more people are working on computers than cars – "knowledge" jobs are proliferating. This shift is changing how we live, how we educate our children, how we plan our careers and how our workplace functions.

The most important and dramatic change of the late 20th century has been the shift to the post-industrial or New Knowledge Economy. The raw material for this economy is no longer steel or coal but information. Of the four economic ages we've experienced, the New Knowledge Economy has called for the most rapid adjustments. The first economic age was agricultural, and it was remarkably long-lived – farming began sometime in 10,000 B.C. It was only 200 years ago that the Industrial Revolution took place, moving us towards a Mass Production Economy. That transformation took about 50 years. A Pre-Industrial Craft Economy straddled the agricultural and industrial ages, but by the time the Industrial Revolution was over, the independent village craftsman had become the city factory worker.

THINKING FOR A LIVING

Today, a conservative estimate would place 80 percent of the workforce in the knowledge and service worker sector, with only 20 percent remaining in the manufacturing sector. More people than ever before in the history of the world are "thinking for a living." As a direct result of the information explosion and the advent of the New Knowledge Economy in the last ten years, society and the workplace have literally started to re-invent themselves. With little precedent to guide us, the world has become an increasingly complex place.

At work, traditional hierarchies and bureaucracies, built like the Egyptian pyramids to last forever, have now begun to crumble. Even the distinctions of title, task and department are blurring. A new 1990s organizational structure is taking shape, flatter and federated with fewer layers of management – the model of interdependence.

Management structures were once external to the dependent worker. The keys to success were power, order, predictability and control. But as technology, the accompanying information explosion and globalization started to transform the workplace in the 1980s, increasingly empowered individuals gained independence. In the past, the individual was "trapped" inside the management structure at work. Now, each individual must build their own internal management structure. Self-management has become more than just a buzzword. It is one key to survival in the new business world.

It's becoming clear now, though, that the autonomous worker or organization can no longer keep pace with the massive amount of change and new information. The final goal of management should be to reach a state of interdependence – the highest and most effective level. That's why we're seeing teamwork take on such importance in the workplace today. Interestingly enough, interdependence between empowered, independent, self-managed individuals is not only a viable goal to strive for in the workplace; interdependence is also the key to successful family and global relations. There is much to be gained from working with other individuals and organizations to achieve common goals.

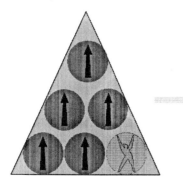 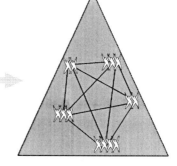

Dependence   Independence   Interdependence

TSUNAMI OF CHANGE

In past economies, there was little need to be a Priority Manager. The formula for life was simple– get an education, find a job, work hard, get married, have a family. The payoff seemed simple too– happiness and security. Today, that's the stuff of fairytales. The tsunami – or tidal wave – of change washing over every aspect of our lives has, in just over a decade, swept away many of these old truths and left millions searching for new anchors.

People are working longer and harder to cope with global competition, the overwhelming volume of information crossing their desks and a faster-paced work environment. During the past decade, our working hours have increased by 20 percent, while our leisure time has decreased by 32 percent. A recent Priority Management survey, *The 21st Century Workplace,* found that stress levels are at an all time high. Most managers experience stress regularly and almost half report feeling stress every day. Technological innovations were supposed to make us more efficient and release us from mundane tasks, spawning a society with adequate time for leisure. In fact, they've had the opposite effect.

It's become vital that we learn how to manage not only our time, but our priorities. The loss of control all these changes have wrought in many people's lives is devastating. There are some who try to convince themselves they're managing well when they're merely crisis managing -- lurching from one urgent development to another with no time for reflection, for LIFE, in between. Our lives cry out for balance, and yet few can identify, let alone practice, the skills needed to bring things under control.

It is only by becoming a Priority Manager that you can learn to be more productive, less stressed and significantly more balanced in every important aspect of your life, not just in the workplace. That's because being a Priority Manager means using a values-based way of making decisions and prioritizing your time. Your priorities can change. Your values and principles don't. These are the only remaining anchors after the tsunami of change has swept away every other touchstone.

Values-based management ties into time management. It is the recognition that at 5:30 p.m. your priorities can shift radically, depending on your values and personal goals. It means that getting home to a friend or spouse, making it to your daughter's softball game or fitting in a leisurely run can become just as important as a meeting or cocktails with clients. It is also the recognition that YOU, the individual, have to make that decision, because nobody else will do it for you. As the saying goes, "If it's to be, it's up to me."

As most of us have experienced first-hand, it's not only the workplace that has seen massive changes. Family structures and dynamics have also altered substantially – all the more reason to learn to manage your whole life, not just your work life. Remember Beaver Cleaver's family? Mr. Cleaver went to work each day and Mrs. Cleaver stayed home with the kids. That was family life in the 1950s.

Today, you would have a hard time finding that kind of family outside of nostalgic TV re-runs. Now just one in ten families fits the mold of the "traditional" or nuclear family. There is no longer one dominant model of family life. Single-parent households, working mothers, stay-at-home dads and blended families resulting from remarriage are all more or less common.

Probably the most significant social change in recent years has been the massive entry of women into the workforce. As a result, men and women now must constantly juggle the pressures of their work with their family responsibilities. Family crises – the child with a broken arm, the brother needing financial help – can never be anticipated or scheduled. What you can do is become adept at prioritizing these needs as they arise.

Interestingly, at the same time that the nuclear family is in decline as the most common model of family life, there is a resurgence in the importance people are placing on family – in whatever configuration. In the international survey of business people, *The 21st Century Workplace*, Priority Management asked individuals what would make them happier in the year 2000. The number one answer? More time with the family.

THE 21ST CENTURY WORKPLACE

The office looks very different in the 1990s than it did just a decade ago. It's not only the internal structures such as management that have changed, but the external ones, too. Computers and faxes are now standard items and workstations have been reshaped accordingly. For some, the workplace has moved to the home as record numbers of people start small businesses. Recognizing the benefits of technology, a generation of New Rustics is leaving the corporate maze and setting up "electronic cottages" in record numbers.

In the transformed workplace of the New Knowledge Economy, white collar productivity has become difficult to measure. The 1980s microchip gurus trumpeted a productivity revolution in the workplace, with computer technology leading the charge. But in fact, the technological developments of the 1980s did little to improve the productivity of white collar workers. Faced with a daily bombardment of information in the form of faxes, telephone calls, overnight packages, electronic mail and office interruptions, knowledge workers – from upper management to clerical assistants – have trouble staying focussed. They try to juggle too many tasks at once, rarely distinguishing between urgent and important. This frenzy of activity is a poor substitute for actually getting the right things accomplished.

The skills you learn today as a Priority Manager will carry you through into the 21st century. To be successful in the year 2000 means knowing that both the right *tools* and *processes* are needed in order to become a Priority Manager. The processes of knowledge work are complex, but essential. They begin with the end – that is to say, the most important process is fixing a purpose, goal or outcome in your mind and then backing up to decide what steps will take you there. This can apply to goals you set in every area of your life; from a new product launch at work, to that tree house you're building for the kids, to working up to your personal best in next month's half-marathon.

As we mature as knowledge workers, there is a pressing need for new kinds of tools to aid thinking, decision-making, planning and communication. It is these tools that will allow people to take maximum advantage of the opportunities which will arise in the years ahead.

Consider the differences between the factory and the office as we move from a blue collar to a white collar workforce. The factory is the place where people make things for a living. The office is the place where people think for a living. Productivity has increased in the factory, by making the best use of tools and improving the processes of production. At the office, we've been busy acquiring tools – computers, software and the like – and then trying to find work to match them. This has led to a massive white collar productivity gap.

A tool is something that works the raw material – a circular saw splits logs, turning them into boards; a hammer pounds a nail, attaching one board to another. If the raw material is tangible, it's easy to devise the right tool. But what about when the raw material is an intangible, like information? You can't see it, taste it, touch it. And yet out of bits of information come expanded ideas and entire concepts and systems.

Now, consider the office as a factory. A place brimming over with rich raw materials that can be hammered into shape by using the best productivity tool in the world. You're most likely familiar with this hefty three-pound tool. It's called the brain. Corporations have tried to apply the lessons learned in manufacturing by automating the office. But all those capital outlays for information technology have managed to do is speed up communications, increase our ability to transmit (and receive!) more information and replace a few dull, repetitive tasks. Until the day technology can improve our creativity and ability to innovate, we must continue to rely on our own three-pound tool for complex knowledge work.

RULES FOR TOOLS

There are some basic rules for tools:

1) A tool must do the job with the minimum effort, complexity and power. Ask yourself, "What is the simplest, smallest, lightest, easiest tool for the job?"

2) The tool must serve the work – the work doesn't exist for the sake of the tool.

3) Tools are extensions of people. They extend the capacity of the body – such as a hammer which increases strength.

The Priority Manager personal organizer has been developed with these three rules in mind. It is an extension of your mind – complex information handling and cross-referencing in a user-friendly format. *The Priority Manager* is designed to act as a bridge between the work and the worker. The system is really a myriad tools in one. It's a day, week, month and year planner, communications planner, activities planner, project planner and meetings planner.

But above all, it's a priorities planner – a tool to help you put your value system to work in order to lead a more balanced life. It's the essential tool to have with you at all times as you undertake your journey to become a Priority Manager. The journey into a future where you have control.

SHOOTING THE RAPIDS

*"Profound and powerful forces are shaking and remaking our world…
The urgent question of our time is whether we can make change
our friend and not our enemy."*

1993 U.S. PRESIDENTIAL INAUGURAL ADDRESS

It is clear that our world is in a total state of flux. The Information Big Bang and the ongoing changes in technology, the workplace, the family and society that have accompanied it mean that we're continually confronted by permanent whitewater, with no calm stretches. And there isn't an end in sight. We are all being challenged to shoot the rapids of constant change – to become *whitewater managers*.

Some people instinctively avoid change. It makes them uncomfortable, disrupts the order of their lives and forces them to deal with the unknown. But avoiding change is no longer an option. Any Priority Manager knows that only by embracing life-long learning can you stay competitive in a continually changing environment. To paraphrase the Duke of Wellington: Wise people learn when they can; fools learn when they must.

If you tend to equate rapid change with a state of crisis, stop and reflect on the Chinese symbols for the word crisis: Wei Ji. Wei spells "danger," while Ji means "opportunity." You must realize that change is here to stay – indeed it is the only constant – and decide how you're going to confront it. As a crisis, simply focussing on the danger and trying not to get wet? Or as an opportunity, catching the biggest wave and riding it into the future? A Priority Manager would choose the latter.

Wēi
(Danger)

Jī
(Opportunity)

As you undertake your own personal Odyssey to become a Priority Manager, it's important to remember that the road isn't particularly smooth and simple. No odyssey ever is. Just as Homer's hero Ulysses encountered various obstacle courses during his ten long years of wandering to get back home, you will, too, as you begin to hone a self-management style that lets you "get back home" – to yourself, to your family, to your values.

And just like the sage and inventive Ulysses, you'll be able to negotiate your way through those obstacle courses and negotiate the rapids without hitting rocks.

Each of the following chapters presents a major hurdle to overcome and its accompanying solutions. **The Time Crunch** shows you how to cope with the sometimes mind-numbing demands on your time. **The Decision Dilemma** helps you conquer the urge to deal solely with the urgent. **The Balancing Act** outlines how you can use your value system as an anchor to bring your home and work personas into synch. **20/20 Memory** puts an end to ineffective communication and delegation. **The Stress Factor** offers more than an ounce of prevention, and suggests that sometimes there's no need for cure.

In **Choice, Not Chance**, you will negotiate perhaps the most formidable obstacle of all – the unplanned future – and discover that the Odyssey to becoming a Priority Manager is a lifelong adventure. And finally, in **The Effectiveness Challenge**, you'll be given a glimpse of the challenges and solutions that lie ahead in the 21st century workplace.

THE TIME CRUNCH

The clock, not the steam-engine, is the key machine
of the modern industrial age.

LEWIS MUMFORD

SEVERAL YEARS AGO, THE TIME CRUNCH
had Cam MacIntyre in a headlock. The president of Cammac Financial Services in Ottawa, Canada, he found there never seemed to be enough hours in the day. When that was compounded by interruptions from colleagues and myriad telephone calls, he couldn't control his daily schedule.

"It was like the tail wagging the dog, instead of the dog wagging the tail," he says.

What Cam MacIntyre needed to start doing was managing his time, and that included interruptions from others as well as his self-imposed distractions. His problem was hardly unique – "never enough time!" seems to be the rallying cry of business people worldwide.

The steam-engine may have long been out-distanced by the jet plane and satellite technology, but the clock continues to reign supreme. Time's iron-fisted rule over our lives appears unshakable. If the 1970s were the Me Decade and the 1980s the Greed Decade, then the 1990s are well on their way to being christened the Time Crunch Decade.

DREAMING OF A 25-HOUR DAY

Even the planet earth can effectively complete its rotation in 24 hours (it actually takes 23 hours, 56 minutes and 4 seconds). Many people wish it took a little longer, that there was another hour in each day. The Values Gap, one of Priority Management's international surveys, found that professionals feel the time crunch acutely. Longer work days have resulted in less time for other activities –

for family, friends, community, spiritual reflection and for ourselves. Then, gridlocked by overcrowded highways and streets in prolonged commutes, you return home in a state of high stress. Another Priority Management study found that 48 percent of respondents suffer from stress every single day.

It might be a cliché, but "too much to do, too little time" is how most adults view their lives today. Priority Management research has found that most people work extra hours on a regular basis:

- 85% work 45 hours per week or more
- 83% work through lunch at least once a week
- 65% work at least one weekend a month

These findings have been borne out by other major North American surveys, one of which found at least one-third of the population continually trying to do more than they could handle. On average, people would like to reduce their workday by about an hour and fifteen minutes, according to The Values Gap. But there's a catch. They'd still like to accomplish the same amount of work.

That may sound like an unlikely proposition, but for a Pritority Manager it's altogether possible. The first step is to recognize why you're spending so much time at work. And then to do something about it.

THE TIME BANDITS

That coveted hour and a quarter a day would be easier to recoup if it wasn't for all the time bandits that sneak up on us during the course of each working day. The time crunch may look like a formidable obstacle, but if you examine its components, you'll find that they're all hurdles that can be overcome.

Over the years, Priority Management has identified a number of top productivity problems common from Sydney, Australia to Sydney, Nova Scotia. They are universal office problems that pop up during any discussion with frustrated knowledge workers. Some of them – crisis management, lack of priorities, attempting too much, and ineffective delegation – will be dealt with in subsequent chapters. Right now, let's look at one of the more insidious enemies of productivity: interruptions.

Priority Management's research indicates managers actually spend almost three hours a day dealing with interruptions. There are two kinds of interruptions. Silent interruptions are the insidious ones that first appear harmless. Noisy interruptions include the phone and your colleagues.

Silent interruptions come in three forms: Mind Traffic, The Paper Chase and Desk Mess.

Mind traffic is an invisible but dangerous interruption. Do you often find yourself at your desk only in body, while your mind has left the room? We've all drifted off during the course of a task to fret about future 'to dos' or things we should have done yesterday. To accomplish anything at all during the course of the day, you need to eliminate all the clutter from your mind.

There are two ways to eliminate mind traffic: do it, or write it down. If doing it immediately is out of the question, remember that your mind will complete about 90 percent of an activity if you write it down somewhere your mind trusts. Using telephone slips, sticky notes, scraps of paper or your last business card is the wrong way to get rid of mind traffic. All you'll end up doing is shuffling little notes around and accomplishing nothing.

The right way to write it down, is to use your Priority Manager personal organizer. By transferring 'to dos', upcoming meetings and incompletions to the appropriate page of your personal organizer, you will relieve the stress and anxiety created by mind traffic. Then, on the day you've planned to complete that activity... Do It!

The paper chase results from trying to eliminate mind traffic by transferring all your thoughts to different pieces of paper. Indeed, some of us have become note junkies. And in addition to self-created paper talk, there are all those phone messages, reports, newspapers and magazines you've vowed to read, and letters to be answered – all screaming, "Look at me!" Research shows three percent of documents are misfiled, and it costs an average of $200 to recover each misfiled document. Paper talk can become a serious condition and lead to terminal deskstress, so these two silent interrupters can be dealt with at the same time.

Desk mess is the most visible and obvious outward sign of productivity problems. A cluttered desk may be considered a sign of genius, but a clean desk is the starting point for improving productivity. At any one time, the average manager's desk holds 36 hours of work. There is a mistaken belief that if work is in front of you, it will get done. Instead, work piles up on the your desk and confusion sets in. Managers spend an average of three hours a week simply looking for things on their desks. Now, that's a time waster.

A common denominator of top executives is that they all work from a clean desk. They can't afford to sit and look at billion dollar headaches all day long. You, too, can get into the habit of starting the day working from a clean desk by following the 4-Ds to eliminating desk mess:

- Do it now

- Decide to do it later

- Delegate it

- Discard

Remove all items from your desk. Your in-box should be put out of sight in an accessible drawer – only your secretary and one or two other people need to know where it is. Then work through the 4 Ds. Decide how much of the material can feasibly be acted on immediately and what should be scheduled for another time. You'll want to time-activate some of it as "to dos" on the Activity pages of your personal organizer. Once you've "decided when", identify what can be delegated. We'll take a look at the art of delegation in Chapter 5.

The next step is to discard whatever possible. Finally, file everything out of sight. It's a good idea to create three holding files to keep close at hand – mail/correspondence; reading; and project/miscellaneous. When you time-activate, don't forget to put a reference as to where you've filed things on your Activities page. This will save some of the 15 to 40 percent of the day which knowledge workers spend seeking and gathering information.

There's another silent time waster that afflicts most knowledge workers at one time or another – procrastination. Webster's Dictionary defines procrastination as "putting off intentionally and habitually" what could (and should!) be done today. Some people do it out of insecurity, because they fear failure. Others are perfectionists who always seek more information before starting a job. Then there are those who do it because they haven't learned to endure short-term pain for long-term gain.

Many of us tend to do the easy tasks first, ("majoring in the minors") just so we feel as if we're getting something done. Then we're left with the more difficult work which begins to take on a formidable appearance. But waiting only invites guilt and stress, which wastes even more time and energy and makes the project all the more difficult. Learn to overcome the temptation of doing the easiest, and usually less important, jobs first.

Being organized is the first step towards overcoming procrastination. Learn to organize your time, your records and even your interruptions. Planning is essential. At the end of each work day, evaluate what you've accomplished that day and review your schedule for the following day. Be decisive about things – just as with desk mess, you have to decide when to do, discard or delegate a task. Clearing your desk will also help solve procrastination problems.

Dealing with noisy interruptions requires more tact than dealing with the silent ones, because these involve other people. Noisy interruptions usually consist of co-workers, drop-in visits, meetings, socializing and, of course our friend, the telephone.

Interruptions by co-workers are unavoidable when you work in an office. But you can prevent these interruptions from becoming major time wasters that derail you from what's important. Here are several techniques you can use to deal with interruptions by colleagues, subordinates and even supervisors. Try establishing "office hours" – setting aside a regular period of time when you're not to be disturbed. For example, every Thursday afternoon, or 8-9 a.m. daily. This "appointment with yourself" or uninterrupted "A" time is an opportunity to tackle important projects. Or try "bundling" interruptions by scheduling regular meetings with key people and effectively preempting possible interruptions.

Take control of your time and just say, "No". If your current task is a higher priority than the subject of the interruption, schedule time later in the day for the interruption. That way you stay on track without alienating co-workers. Or you can try standing up. Stand up meetings take only 75 percent of the time of sit down meetings. Another technique is to encourage co-workers to stop and question the necessity or validity of an interruption. And do others the courtesy of practising this yourself.

Meetings can be a dead-zone for workplace productivity. Most managers spend too much time in too many meetings – for too few results. According to Priority Management research, the average manager spends more than 11 hours a week in meetings. But as much as 25 percent of that time is wasted. You can substantially cut time spent in meetings by forward-planning. Chapter 5 takes an in depth look at meeting management.

The telephone is our greatest communication tool, but sometimes it seems like our greatest enemy. Make use of voice-mail and fax to avoid time-consuming rounds of telephone tag. And buy yourself periods of uninterrupted work by having phone calls held, making sure to specify when you can be reached. Another telephone tactic is to be truthful and admit you don't have time. Or start the conversation by stating: "In a few minutes I have to ____, can we cover this quickly?"

Like the telephone, technology can both aid and hinder our productivity, adding to the flow of our daily interruptions. Not long ago, we received mail only once a day. Today, fax machines, overnight air couriers and electronic mail bombard us with messages by the minute. As we become more accustomed to new technologies, it will be easier to deal with interruptions. For example, we're starting to realize that just because a message arrives by fax or modem, it doesn't necessarily merit immediate attention. Like any message, it can be prioritized.

Technology is also a productivity problem if you don't know how to use it properly. A lack of understanding greatly impedes productivity. By becoming technologically literate, you can make technology work for you and not against you.

Cam McIntrye started using The Priority Manager seven years ago, and since then he's been effectively "wagging his own tail." His personal organizer allows him to control his time and interruptions. He's frank with colleagues, telling them he just doesn't have time when he's unnecessarily interrupted. And to back up his claim, he shows them the Plan and Activities pages of his Priority Manager. They invariably back off.

He also sticks to an undisturbed "office hour" every day between 9 and 10 a.m., during which he returns phone calls and makes time for his own important calls. Using his Priority Manager to control his time is one of the reasons Cam MacIntrye has doubled his earnings of seven years ago. And he still finds time to teach aerobics classes during the day.

Learning to control silent and noisy interruptions frees up valuable and productive time. Research shows that after Priority Management training, unnecessary interruptions are reduced by 26 percent. But on your Odyssey to becoming a Priority Manager, managing time is only the preliminary step. A satisfying and big step, granted, and one that means you're ready to confront even larger obstacles.

WHAT IS YOUR TECHNO-QUOTIENT?

Rapid technological developments have created productivity problems for many in the workplace today. There are huge gaps in technology literacy, and this lack of understanding is both a major time-waster and an obstacle to productivity. Rate your "techno-quotient".

1) On a daily basis, do you use a:

computer	__Yes	__ No
fax	__Yes	__ No
modem	__Yes	__ No
car telephone	__Yes	__ No
voice mail	__Yes	__ No

2) Do you compose documents on your computer, rather than by hand? __Yes __ No

3) Do you know how to use all the features on your telephone? __Yes __ No

4) Do you know how to use all the features on your fax machine? __Yes __ No

5) Have you ever trained someone on how to use a computer or particular software program? __Yes __ No

6) Are you familiar with all the capabilities of your current computer program? __Yes __ No

7) Have you set the time of your VCR, rather than letting it blink 12:00? __Yes __ No

8) Are you able to pre-program your VCR? __Yes __ No

9) Do you know how to use all the functions on your microwave?   __Yes __ No

10) Does your regular reading include articles or publications about
    technology?   __Yes __ No

11) Do you know how to back up your computer files?   __Yes __ No

12) Do you think technological developments will help you do your job,
    rather than threaten it?   __Yes __ No

HOW DO YOU RATE?

Score two points for each Yes answer and one point for each No.

16-22 points: Are you suffering from techno-phobia? Whether you're ready or not, we're entering the Information Age. Start catching up, and get good training to give you a solid foundation.

23-27 points: Don't be complacent! You are coping with technology, but you're still working for it. By learning more, you can discover how technology can work for you.

28-32 points: You're riding the crest of the wave into the Information Age! By maintaining this high level of knowledge and interest, you are well positioned for success. Just make sure you don't become a techie, who is fascinated with "the latest" in technology. Continually ask yourself, is this technology improving my effectiveness or do I go looking for work for my latest techno-toy?

THE DECISION DILEMMA

I do not believe in a fate that falls on men however they act;
but I do believe in a fate that falls on them unless they act.

G.K. CHESTERTON

SHIRLEY MAILLARD ALWAYS CONSIDERED

herself a good juggler – an organized person who knew how to manage her time. What she hadn't counted on when she accepted an important administrative position at a large North American university was that her well-honed time management skills simply wouldn't be enough.

"Crisis management seemed to be the operational way of the university, and that just kept increasing exponentially," Shirley recalls. Her own position was ill-defined. She held a large and varied portfolio, and it seemed that every urgent matter that arose was funnelled her way. Her schedule – daily, weekly, monthly – kept being thrown into chaos. Shirley found herself continually reacting, with precious little time left for acting.

What Shirley Maillard needed to do, as do others who find themselves in a crisis management milieu, was to start managing her priorities. Priority Managers know how to move beyond activity planning and on to priority planning – only then can they start making effective decisions about how to use their time productively.

The information explosion – along with the immeasurable changes it engenders in our work and family lives, and in society as a whole – means the number of decisions we face daily have mushroomed. This has given birth to a syndrome called the "decision dilemma". Many people feel ill-equipped to cope with the demands of decision-making in the ever-changing New Knowledge Economy.

Decisions are made every single minute of the day. Would you believe we make well over 1,000 decisions each day? We only remember making about 200 – the rest happen at an almost subconscious level. All of these decisions may seem to overwhelm us at times. The Massachusetts Institute of Technology has found that we have 600 percent more information to manage today than we did just 20 years ago.

But however many decisions we make, however much information we must process, the real issue is always, "What am I going to do next?" The most frustrating thing is that "What's next?" often seems to be determined by other people.

The way people make choices – decisions – can be looked at as a pyramid. At the bottom lie procrastination and indecision – the ineffectual non-choices. Next come impulse decisions. These are often made hurriedly at the last minute simply because a decision must be made. Then there's a whole middle-layer of decision-making brought on by pressure from others – from superiors, colleagues, clients and outside agencies. This is followed by habit – making the same choices over and over again, because that's the path of least resistance. At the top of the pyramid sit conscious choices, the sole kinds of decisions a Priority Manager should be making.

HIERARCHY OF CHOICES

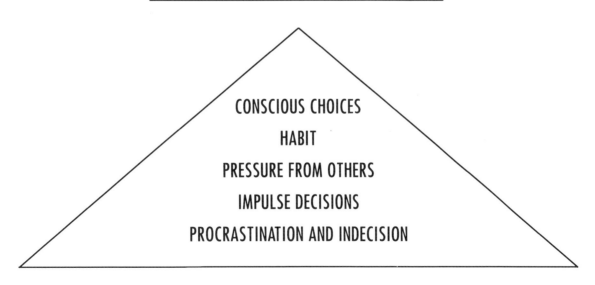

CONSCIOUS CHOICES

HABIT

PRESSURE FROM OTHERS

IMPULSE DECISIONS

PROCRASTINATION AND INDECISION

REACTING ISN'T ACTING

We all know that valuable lessons can be learned from history. Consider the story of Charles Schwab, the president of Bethlehem Steel in the United States in the early 1900s. He was the first American ever to make a salary of one million dollars per annum. Schwab wanted to be even more successful so he consulted with a man called Ivy Lee – the leading management guru of his day.

After observing Schwab's work habits for five days, Lee advised him to take three steps to make himself more productive. Ivy Lee told Charles Schwab:

1) Make a 'to-do' list.

2) Set priorities.

3) Do it every day.

Schwab didn't know what he should pay Lee for this simple three-step advice. Lee told him to work the plan for a while and then pay him what he thought it was worth. Five weeks later, Lee received a check for $25,000 from Schwab. (Remember, this was more than 80 years ago!) Later in his career, Charles Schwab claimed that Ivy Lee's advice was the best he'd been given in his business career, and that it helped him build Bethlehem Steel into the second largest steel producer in the U.S.

The first of Ivy Lee's steps is a given for anyone seeking to be a Priority Manager. But what happens to your 'to do' list when there are time conflicts or new tasks are suddenly thrown into the mix by others? That's when you realize that unless you set priorities, following your 'to-do' list could become as effective as raking autumn leaves in a windstorm – well-intentioned, no doubt, but a lost cause. Priority planning allows you to make decisions that are based on conscious choice.

There are six concrete results of priority planning:

1) It brings control to your life.

2) Through priority planning, you can organize your business, personal and social activities, helping you get the different spheres of your life into synch.

3) It helps you to avoid crisis management.

4) By priority planning you'll become adept at handling incomplete projects and activities, reducing the time you spend playing catch-up.

5) It leads to reduced procrastination and indecision.

6) Finally, but not least importantly, it gives you a manageable workload.

Getting your life under control requires priority management as opposed to crisis management. And learning to make conscious choices means you'll spend less time dashing from crisis to crisis – it will even help you redefine exactly what constitutes a crisis. Often crises are defined by others. But someone else's crisis may not necessarily be yours. Remember that planning means bringing the future into the present so that you can do something about it now.

URGENCY: THE WORKPLACE TYRANT

When colleagues, subordinates and even superiors come towards you waving a project folder or memo, the word "Urgent" already on their lips, you have to honestly ask yourself: "Is the building next door on fire?" That's because what other people consider to be urgent often isn't really important enough to override what you're already hard at work on.

But there are those times when the crisis genuinely appears to be valid. That's the kind of situation Shirley Maillard found herself in at the university. What Shirley felt she needed was a tool to help her manage her time around various crises. She also wanted to learn how to extrapolate from each crisis in order to develop strategic plans – ones that would allow her to move beyond mere activities planning. She wanted to start acting instead of reacting.

She found that tool in The Priority Manager and has been using her personal organizer for five years to determine daily, weekly and monthly what is important and what is merely urgent. Shirley has learned that if time is made for important activities, fewer things reach the point where they boil over to the "Urgent!" stage.

Control begins with planning – planning your life, your month, your week and your day. Only then can you begin turning your intentions into actions. Most of us get caught up in an activity trap. We think that if we're busy all the time we're achieving something. Very few people sit back, look at their lives and ask, "What do I want to do? What do I want to achieve?" Even fewer go on to do the things that will help them achieve their goals.

That's because most people are merely activity managers instead of priority managers. All knowledge work begins with output. We have to know where we're going before we can get out of the starting blocks. So it's not enough to simply list all the activities you need to do. You have to examine which of those activities are leading to a specific goal. Otherwise you'll spend a great deal of your time doing unproductive tasks.

WORK VALUE MATRIX

	IMPORTANCE		VALUE
	M1 DIRECT VALUE High importance High urgency	M2 INDIRECT VALUE High importance Low urgency	
	M3 NECESSARY NON-VALUE High urgency Low importance	M4 UNNECESSARY NON-VALUE Low urgency Low importance	

URGENCY

There are four types of work, with varying degrees of importance. First there is **Direct Value**, which shows immediate rewards, such as meeting a deadline for a sales proposal or mowing the lawn. Next is **Indirect Value**—tasks such as planning and learning which bear fruit down the road. Tasks defined as **Necessary Non-value** include filling out your tax return or completing a report for your boss—activities that must be done but provide you with little in the way of rewards. In the final quadrant there is **Unnecessary Non-value.** This is looking for files you've lost on your desk, playing "telephone tag" or rearranging your sock drawer.

The key is to devote more of your energy to the M2 quadrant, Indirect Value. Try to eliminate activities in M3 and M4, which are often "B" priorities but which often take precedence if you are trying to avoid the important tasks at hand.

Important activities are those which have an incremental effect. By getting them done, you move increasingly closer to your goals. Urgent activities demand immediate attention, usually because someone – either yourself, a colleague, a subordinate, or a superior – has planned poorly. Many people "major in the minors" all their lives because they can't distinguish between important and urgent.

Those who do the most, don't always get the most done. This is known as the Pareto Principle. Vilfredo Pareto was a turn-of-the-century Italian economist and sociologist living in Switzerland. He fathered the 80/20 principle. What it means for us as knowledge workers is that a mere 20 percent of the things we do daily create 80 percent of our results. The other 80 percent consists of hollow, ineffective activities that usually amount to reacting to the urgent, or make-work projects. Activity for activity's sake.

At the very heart of priority planning is a built-in mechanism for the value of your work, by distinguishing between important and urgent activities. Priority Managers learn how to divide their days' activities into 'As' and 'Bs' – in other words, priorities and non-priorities. It is vital that you can distinguish between the two. You'd be surprised how many people can't.

The 'As' are made up of a number of important activities. First there are your commitments and promises. These apply both to your business and personal lives. Don't ever break a commitment. One Priority Management client learned this the hard way.

This businessman had made a note on the Plans page of his *Priority Manager* that he had an appointment with his son, to take him fishing in the evening. When he got home after work that day, they gathered up the gear and got into the car, his son in what appeared to be a state of nervous excitement. By the time they got to the end of the street, his son had burst into tears in the back seat. The father pulled over to the curb and turned around, concerned. "What's the matter, son?" Through his tears, the boy said, "I thought you were going to cancel like you did all the other times."

A commitment is always an 'A'. Otherwise, the personal and professional repercussions are enormous – you could lose the trust of important people. Other 'As' include items leading to major goals and Long-term Value tasks. Anything which helps you accomplish your monthly and yearly objectives should be designated an 'A'. The third type of 'As' are your 'must-dos.' These are the things that are unavoidable and if you don't do them today, it will be too late tomorrow.

The 'Bs' are all the items that are not critical to that particular day, are not previous commitments and don't lead incrementally to long-range goals. A 'B' can wait until tomorrow. Don't even consider undertaking a 'B' activity until you have tackled all your 'As', although if left on the backburner long enough, some 'Bs' can become 'As'.

Once you've filled in your Activities page, designating items either 'A' or 'B', look through the list and decide which of the items can be delegated. For example, perhaps there are travel arrangements to be made for a business trip the following week. This is the kind of task that can be handled by a trusted secretary or assistant.

After deciding what can be delegated, you can now go ahead and sequence the remaining activities – in order of importance, not the order you intend to do them. For example, 'A1' is 'A1' even if you do it at the end of the day. This will help keep your results achievement-oriented.

Once you've designated, delegated and ordered your activities, it's time to set your eye on the clock. We all tend to underestimate how long things take. For example, the average business call is more than three minutes in duration, and that includes the 70 percent of calls during which only messages are left.

Time estimates are important because they allow you to determine whether or not you're attempting too much, which is one of the leading stress factors in business life. Estimating how long all your activities will take will leave you with a realistic number of 'As' and 'Bs'. Here's a tip: add a minimum of 25 percent extra time on your 'As' to allow for interruptions, which occur about every eight minutes on average.

Priority Managers know where their time goes. They continually diagnose how they're spending their time and are quick to prune unproductive activities. They concentrate their time and effort on what's important. And they leave room for the unexpected by building cushions of time around every major task.

The crucial thing to remember is that Priority Managers use a value-based way of designating priorities. Your 'As' and 'Bs' don't exist in a vacuum, as the businessman who kept promising to take his son fishing realized. Your personal organizer will only be doubly effective if you take a whole-life approach in using it. Your Activities page should include items that relate to your work, home and social lives. The following chapter will detail the importance of balance in a successful Priority Manager's life.

A value-based approach is the only way to break free of the decision dilemma syndrome. For difficult decisions, you have to go back to your value system and act accordingly. That will put you at the top of the decision-making pyramid. You will be making conscious choices. Anything less than that means you're making choices for the wrong reasons and putting your behavior into conflict with your personal values.

Our values are the deep-seated conclusions and beliefs about things that are important to us. To be effective, you need to become a 'values manager'. A values manager – or Priority Manager – knows how to do the right things, rather than just doing things right. What this amounts to is the difference between being effective or merely being efficient.

Efficient workers are content to simply cross items off their daily 'to-do' lists – the more items the better.

An effective worker, a Priority Manager that is, considers the relative importance of the completed activities. To be described as "an efficient worker" in the 1990s is not the compliment it once was. It's somewhat akin to commending a gardener who cuts the lawn quickly, but in the process mows down all the flowerbeds in his path.

Overcoming the decision dilemma syndrome by managing your priorities in a value-based way puts you farther along the road on your Odyssey to becoming a Priority Manager. Just as Ulysses couldn't turn back after making his way unharmed past the Scylla, a deadly six-headed beast, learning to make conscious choices means you're also closer to "making it home."

ARE YOU EFFICIENT OR EFFECTIVE?

In today's workplace, it's not enough to be efficient. You could complete ten tasks in a morning, but if they aren't important, your time might not have been well spent. You have to be effective, which means getting the right things done. Take this quiz to determine whether your working style leans more towards "efficient" or "effective".

1) When the mail arrives, do you look through it immediately to make sure you aren't missing something that needs action? __Yes __No

2) When a fax crosses your desk, do you read it right away? __Yes __No

3) When someone asks for your help with something, do you pride yourself on being able to respond immediately? __Yes __No

4) Do you judge how successful your day was by counting how many items are crossed off your "to do" list without considering their relative importance? __Yes __No

5) Do you often get to the end of the day and find you haven't made "an appointment with yourself"—a solid period of uninterrupted time? __Yes __No

6) Do you try to respond to phone messages immediately, even if it interrupts something else? __Yes __No

7) Do you find that some days you don't even look at your "to do" list until several hours into the work day? __Yes __No

HOW DO YOU RATE?

Give yourself two points for each Yes answer and one point for each No.

12-14 points: Stop reacting and start managing your priorities! You may put too much emphasis on responding quickly, rather than assessing which tasks are the most important. Don't mistake "urgent" for "important"!

9-11 points: Resist the temptation to react to interruptions, whether it's a fax, mail, phone message or co-worker with a question. If you aren't getting the right things done, you won't win any points for responding quickly to less important demands on your time.

7-8 points: Congratulations! You probably know how to identify and manage your priorities. This helps you focus your energies most productively. Remember to prioritize every task, so you can determine which ones should command your attention first.

THE BALANCING ACT

The goal of war is peace;
of business leisure.

ARISTOTLE, POLITICS IV

It was about four years ago that

Scott Harris took his own version of the Tombstone Test. And Scott, the owner of Mustang Marketing and Advertising in Agoura Hills, California, was not pleased with the results.

Things were going well at work, but that was because he was putting in 80 to 90 hours a week in order to achieve the results he wanted. On the homefront, his four-year-old son had just started playing baseball – one of Scott's own passions – but he hardly had time to take in the games, let alone coach his son's Little League team as he hoped to.

"In my mind there was a clear vision of why I wanted to have kids, but all of the various goals I'd established weren't compatible," he says. "There was a big discrepancy between the things I wanted and the things I was doing."

Scott Harris wasn't watching his son grow up and he also wasn't doing any of the things that used to give him pleasure – playing softball, baseball, golf and tennis. The time for flexibility and spontaneity had disappeared from his life.

Many people, like Scott Harris, wake up one day to find their lives out of balance and don't know what to do about it. Working in the New Knowledge Economy has translated to working more. Since 1973, the amount of time that knowledge workers spend working has increased by 20 percent, while their leisure time has dropped by 32 percent. This sits in striking contrast to the rosy predictions of futurists in the 1950s and 1960s. In those days, many optimistically expected that improved technology and automation would increase leisure time for all.

Priority Management's survey *The Values Gap* found that men and women feel the time crunch equally. Both genders are feeling the same stresses and strains of coping with the hectic and unrelenting pace of work. In addition to these professional demands though, we are all struggling to fulfill personal commitments – to ourselves and to others.

Our lives demand balance, yet few can identify, let alone practice, the skills needed to bring things under control. With all the changes wrought by the information explosion, our values remain the only true anchors in our lives. And it is to these anchors that the Priority Manager must return again and again.

THE VALUES GAP

The values gap is a recent phenomenon, one born out of a response to our changing and challenging world. The information revolution was paralleled by a social revolution – one spearheaded by the re-emergence of personal ideals and values. *The Values Gap* survey found that the majority of people today show a strong desire to return to the values of past generations – with the family at the centre of that shift. Respondents reported a desire for a total of two hours more each day to spend with family and friends, and on community pursuits. Like Scott Harris, they recognize that personal values often conflict with our behavior. After all, it takes time to have a friend, it takes time to love.

The widening gulf between personal and corporate values – the values gap – affects all of us. The major workplace issue of the 1990s is the balancing of personal and corporate values in the face of demands for ever-increasing productivity. But the two need not be at odds. Many of the benefits of future economic development in the New Knowledge Economy, will go to those individuals and companies who realize the integral role personal values play in shaping a new workplace perspective.

The values gap develops when the requirements of the workplace force a compromise with our deeply held beliefs and attitudes. Nowhere is this discrepancy more evident than in the dominant role work plays in determining our leisure time and in limiting the expression of our personal values.

The difference between the current reality and the desired future, creates a disturbing tension for change which workplace attitudes and values are only beginning to reflect. The major victim of the values gap is, without doubt, the family.

The family has borne the bulk of the assault of the changeover from the Mass Production to the New Knowledge Economy. The pace at home now rivals the pace at the office. Children, spouses and parents are as tightly scheduled as the most sophisticated business meeting. The pressures of the values gap can lead to stress on the job, poor relationships and marital breakdowns.

There is a solution – bringing your home and work personas into synch. Evidence suggests that those who have brought their values to the surface and understand them can change things for the better. The most important skill for knowledge workers today is the ability to manage values and priorities. By knowing how to identify our values and manage our lives around them, we work more effectively. By becoming a values manager, or Priority Manager, you can put an out-of-balance life back in control.

The most important step is to acknowledge that the values gap is real and that it affects you and those you care about. The next step is to stop living a Jekyll and Hyde existence and face the fact that you live only one life. That fact should be overwhelmingly evident to anyone who glances at the Plan and Activities pages of your *Priority Manager* personal organizer.

This tool manages your business *and* personal life. Your children's soccer league schedule and school plays, and your racketball games and Sante Fe-style cooking classes, all vie for attention on the same pages as deadlines for new product launches and 4th quarter reports. And don't forget your dental appointments and that state-of-the-art fly fishing rod you've wanted to check out for weeks now. When you're designating activities as 'As or 'Bs', remember that it's not only work-related items that merit an 'A'.

A values manager knows that not all roles and decisions should be financially-based. Make absolutely certain your schedule includes time for family, friends, community and other key expressions

of your values. Remember the Tombstone Test. Regrets later in life usually focus on misspent time –
especially time not spent with children or parents.

If you're finding some of your values at odds with each other, perhaps you need to realign them.
The 1980s were defined by "more." Take a personal stand to make the 1990s the decade of "less." Be
wary of rampant consumerism, which can trap you in a cycle of work-spend-work.

To get your life back in control, strive for balance in six key
areas – work, learning, physical, social, family and spiritual. Just as
all knowledge work begins with output – setting goals and deciding what you must do to take you there – you must decide what
you want to achieve in each of these six areas.

For example, to fulfill yourself intellectually you may decide to
learn everything you can about Post-Modern architecture. To get
yourself there, perhaps you need to enroll in a course. Or you could
choose to do it on your own by reading every available book, or
signing educational videos out of the library and the local archi-
tectural institute. You could even plan a trip to Chicago, the
mecca of Post-Modern architecture – thus combining an intellectual goal with a family vacation or
time alone with your partner.

Priority Managers are already adept time managers and decision-makers. You don't have to be
superhuman to fit in activities involving the six key components of a balanced life. You need to be
aware of their importance, set goals and manage your priorities accordingly.

It was during a Priority Management training course that Scott Harris realized that he could
develop the management skills necessary to realign his values. He modified his work goals and
dramatically reduced his hours by becoming more focussed and hiring extra staff. "I was fairly convinced I was the only one who could do the things that needed to get done," he says. Using his personal
organizer has helped Scott delegate effectively and manage his priorities.

"It's very liberating," he says. "I don't have to remember anything anymore. If it's not in *The
Priority Manager*, it doesn't count. And I have it with me at home and at work."

He doesn't sleep any more than he used to, but his life today brims with outside work activities. He coaches his son's Little League team and has time to spend with his wife and three-year-old daughter. He also teaches reading to advanced students at his son's school on a volunteer basis, has a social life and plays softball, baseball, golf and tennis. By managing his values, Scott Harris has been able to recapture his lost spontaneity.

Scott has successfully managed to transform himself into a Five O'Clock Dad. Remember years ago when the traditional businessman put in his day's work and at 5 p.m. went home to his wife and children? He was no layabout, either – many succeeded in heading up, if not building, sizeable businesses. Sometime during the last two decades, he was bumped aside by fast-tracking baby boomers who found they could move up the corporate ladder faster by logging longer hours. Before long, the extended workday became the expected routine.

But the values revolution of the 1990s is slowly changing all that. As baby boomers start families, they have begun to realize that their corporate success could come at a heavy cost to their family life. They are acknowledging the values gap. Now parents are once again wanting to be Five O'Clock Dads – and Five O'Clock Moms.

As more women enter the workforce, there is less pressure on men to be the sole breadwinners. This has opened up new choices for men – whether to work from home, be a stay-at-home parent or finally take the risk of starting their own business. Working women, now the rule rather than the exception, are finding themselves increasingly timelocked by the demands of work and home. Now we can add to that the newly identified "Daughter Track" – caring for aging parents. Women knowledge workers face a dilemma – although they have become a major force in the workplace, their role as caregiver remains entrenched in the expectations of society.

One of the solutions is to make it clear to your organization, and those at home, that you are working hard at surfacing your values and that their cooperation is vital. No one can realign their values in a vacuum. Both women and men who are learning to be Values or Priority Managers, tend to fare better in a progressive work environment.

This values re-alignment need not come at the expense of your career. As long as productivity is high, superiors will be less likely to gauge performance by the hours logged in the office. Smart corporations are also starting to pay attention to the personal aspects of their employees' lives. They are offering such benefits as counselling in career development, family problems and drug abuse, and "wellness" benefits such as exercise facilities. This is both an investment in human capital, as well as an awareness that professional performance is augmented by a well-balanced personal life.

With the necessary skills and flexibility, business people will be able to remain productive at work while also enjoying family life. The Five O'Clock Moms and Dads will be the new heroes of the 1990s.

THE FIRST MINUTE

Think about how you start your day – your first minute at the office and your first minute at home. These could be the most valuable minutes you'll ever have to spend, and yet you could be squandering them.

Is it your natural inclination to walk into the office and start griping about a report that didn't get finished the previous day or to comment how much work there is still to do? And when you get home, do you immediately begin to grumble and unload everything that went wrong at work that day? Or do you maintain a curt silence? If any of these describe your days perfectly, then you're wasting those precious first minutes.

The first few minutes of anything – a workday, a meeting or an evening at home – set the tenor of everything to come. You can change your entire relationship with people through these initial short encounters.

Let's say you're sitting down in a meeting to deal with the company's annual report. Before getting down to business, focus on the positive. Congratulate someone who got something in before a deadline. Or perhaps comment on the new, provocative cover design that's bound to appeal to shareholders. The mood of the meeting will be positive, despite what sorts of problems and criticisms may later arise. A values manager values other people, respecting their opinions and knowing when to compliment them.

Use this same strategy at home, too. Think about how your kids will remember you years from now. As someone who came home exhausted and crabby every evening, or as a person full of enthusiasm and interesting stories about the work they did? The effects of that first minute are incremental. The positive repercussions add up over the years. They can also breed positive behavior in others, at home and at work.

Like all important strategies with long-range effects, the first minute requires some planning. On your way to work each morning and on your way home each night, take a few moments to plan something nice to say. It sounds so simple, but so few people do it.

Strategic planning is integral to leading a balanced life. Some of it takes no time at all, like planning for the first minute. Other aspects of planning require a bit more thought. The Plan page is the most important page of The Priority Manager. It represents the reality of all our lives: What am I going to do today? How am I going to invest my 86,400 seconds? The Plan page is 24 hours long and is the culmination of all the planning techniques and organizational theory used throughout the system. It brings together our work/home persona, directs us towards balance and achievement, and gives full expression to our values. Eighty percent of the knowledge workers who have trained with Priority Management indicate that they now include personal, social and family activities along with business commitments in their daily plan.

In the bottom right-hand corner of the Plan page you'll find a space for recording the results and achievements of your day. It's important to end every day on a note of achievement. Don't forget to include business, personal and family achievements. Noting your results will give you a sense of accomplishment, make you feel good and be beneficial to your health – thinking positively releases the body's natural 'feel-good' chemicals, endorphins.

Madame Marie Curie once said, "Only the successful end their days asking, 'What did I do well today?'" Too many people sit and wait for someone else to come along and motivate them. You have to motivate yourself. Self-motivation leads to a strong self-image and self-confidence.

In this same space on the Plan page is a screened balance wheel depicting the six facets of a balanced life – work, learning, physical, social, family and spiritual. This is to remind you to look for positives at the end of each day in each facet of your life. You might want to check off areas you feel good about or that you addressed that day. This review will also reveal to you areas you may be neglecting. Remember that it's important to keep score in life, not just in sports. You can be winning but feel like you're losing if you don't keep score.

THE KAROSHI VICTIM VS. THE PLAYAHOLIC

We may often say work is killing us, particularly after a bad week, but in Japan there is increasing concern that overwork may literally be killing people. There's even a name for it – Karoshi. On average, Japanese workers spend as much as 500 more hours on the job annually than do their European counterparts and 200 more than workers in North America, the United Kingdom and Australasia.

Japanese managers are starting to recognize that there are ways to protect their personal health, spend more time with their family and still get the job done. They are now focussing on the importance of balance. This has been encouraged by a government campaign begun in 1989 that urges people to take more time off.

In North America the pendulum appears to be swinging to the other extreme. The fast-tracking workaholics of the 1980s are the new "playaholics" of the 1990s – people who play as hard as they work.

We may be programming ourselves to the point where leisure time is no longer the relaxing and enjoyable break we need from routine. We feel pressured to use our time off as effectively as time on the job. Many people end up rigidly scheduling their weekends – a golf game, followed by a lunch date, tennis and the latest dinner theater performance in the evening. This chronic overscheduling is compounded for playaholics with family demands. They face a full schedule, with little or no free time for spontaneous activities.

When down-time gets filled with more tasks to accomplish, it loses "The 3 R's"—its restorative, recuperative and recreational value. What happens for playaholics is that their weekends can become as overscheduled and exhausting as the work week, because they're cramming in the "leisure" they missed during the week due to overwork. A sub-category of the playaholic is the "obligate exerciser" – a person who no longer works out for fun or health reasons, but because he or she feels obligated to do it.

Our world has become so activity-centred that we no longer have time in our busy lives for reflection, and only through reflection can we recharge our batteries and get our creative juices flowing. In the previous chapter we looked at the danger of confusing activity with achievement. To be creative – to be able to effectively plan your life strategies – you sometimes have to sit back and simply free your mind. If you're rushing from one thing to another, you'll never have time for reflection.

Consider this: a balanced life requires that you plan unplanned time.

Once you've surfaced your values and have begun to re-align them, you're well on your way to a more balanced life – and more than halfway home on your personal Odyssey to becoming a Priority Manager.

ARE YOU A PLAYAHOLIC?

Find out whether your leisure time has become so structured and planned that you are a "playaholic".

1) Have you accumulated vacation time from past years? __ Yes __ No

2) Did you take two weeks vacation or less in the past year? __ Yes __ No

3) Did you feel you had to plan or schedule each holiday day? __ Yes __ No

4) Did you take work with you on your last vacation? __ Yes __ No

5) While on holiday, did you keep in contact with the office by fax or phone? __ Yes __ No

6) Do you prefer to take "active" holidays (skiing, golfing, tennis, hiking or other adventures)? __ Yes __ No

7) Do you prefer to have plans for a weekend day rather than starting the day with no plans? __ Yes __ No

8) Do you frequently feel your time off is too busy? __ Yes __ No

9) Do you rate your weekend by how much you accomplish or how active you were? __ Yes __ No

10) Has your leisure time schedule ever caused you stress? __ Yes __ No

HOW DO YOU RATE?

Give yourself two points for each Yes and one point for each No answer.

17-20 points: You are a playaholic. Get off the treadmill! Make sure your play isn't becoming work and that you can still enjoy unstructured leisure time.

13-17 points: With a little push, you could be a playaholic. Leave the phone at home and allow yourself to do nothing for at least four hours next weekend.

10-13 points: People don't have to tell you to slow down! You are probably more productive at work and happier at home because you're leading a balanced life.

20/20 MEMORY

A fool may talk, but a wise man speaks.

BEN JONSON, 1572-1637

Harry Travis spends a vast amount of

time on the telephone. As vice-president of sales and marketing at a high-tech medical products company in Atlanta, Georgia, he oversees the day-to-day management of a large sales force spread across the U.S. He's on the road a lot himself and does most of his communication via voice mail.

He also manages dozens of small, short term projects that require significant follow-up, as well as some bigger projects – with practically no support staff, as they're all largely in the field.

A couple of years ago, Harry Travis found that even though he was a highly organized person and a committed planner, he was having trouble effectively following up on all of his telephone communications. He realized that it was becoming increasingly difficult to keep track of the mountains of verbal commitments – made by him *and* to him by others.

What Harry Travis was after was 20/20 memory in his communications. He wanted to be able to track who had said what to whom, and to follow-up earlier conversations and voice mail messages accordingly. All Priority Managers know that an integral part of effective communication involves follow-up. The best-laid plans and projects can go awry if communicated poorly or if well-meant verbal commitments are forgotten.

Communication – whether oral, written or technological – represents about 75 percent of a knowledge worker's day. Research shows most of our communication time (55%) is spent listening. Next is speaking at 23% followed by reading at 13% and writing at 8%. As both individuals and organizations learn the value of interdependence in the Information Age, they become aware that finely honed communication skills are more important than ever before. In Priority Management's international survey *The 21st Century Workplace*, respondents named "Communications/Interpersonal

Skills" as the most important skills needed to succeed in business in the future.

With the large degree of change and massive amounts of new information we face regularly, one person simply cannot possess or process all the necessary knowledge or technology needed for a job — hence the need for interdependence. And interdependence means teamwork, which demands good communication skills.

So whether you command a large staff in the office or field, like Harry Travis, or work alongside other independent colleagues, your ability to communicate effectively shouldn't be left to chance. Like most essential management skills, communication skills are not inherent – they can be learned.

There are four components to successful communications of all types. You must plan your communication, capture the responses, follow-up on the responses and be able to store and retrieve the responses, as well as your own follow-up.

The Communication Planners (CPs) in your *Priority Manager* system allow you to deal with all four components on one page. You can plan, record and follow-up on telephone calls, meetings and appointments by using your CPs.

Thoughtfully planning all your communications can save you time and money. For example, one in eight calls generally have to be repeated because the caller forgot something during the course of the conversation. Planned telephone calls are typically five minutes less in duration than unplanned ones. If you make a dozen calls a day, that can add up to sixty minutes saved or wasted – it's up to you. Still dreaming of a 25-hour day? There's your extra hour!

CPs can be used to record one-off phone calls and to follow through on an on-going verbal correspondence – in person and over the telephone. Use the form to keep track of subjects of discussion, as well as the responses you receive. If follow-up is required, you can make note of that and time activate on the appropriate Activities Page. And don't neglect to designate these as 'As'; after all, you've made a commitment.

Many of us often have great ideas to share with key people, ideas that are often forgotten before we get a chance to communicate them. Your CP acts as a proactive communication tool to capture ideas, subjects and questions for future discussion. That way things aren't left to chance and allowed to slip through the cracks.

By using the CPs in his personal organizer, Harry Travis has given himself 20/20 memory in his communications. He has opened a CP on about 15 people he's in contact with regularly and uses his A to Z as a "living filing system." Since he started using the system, Harry Travis made a commitment to himself to log every single telephone call made and received, and has religiously done so. This allows him to plan for the next day, prioritize activities and organize effective follow-up.

"(*The Priority Manager*) is my annex to my brain," he says. "It's amazing how many things I would have missed without this written record."

20/20 memory makes you more productive at work, but it also helps make a difference in other areas of your life. Remember that a Priority Manager knows how to lead a well-balanced life.

A CP should be opened on the people you communicate with the most – including yourself. You can use it as an "ideas" file for personal items, listing titles of books and films people recommend, restaurants you'd like to try and things you'd like to share with your spouse and children. One Priority Management client even opened a CP on his two horses – saving himself time and money by effectively tracking the progress of his expensive hobby.

THE HOT AIR HABIT

Poor communication often translates into "too much talk and no action." Chapter Two looked at noisy interruptions, highlighting meetings as a major time-waster. The reason so many meetings squander our precious time is because of poor communications – before, during and after the meeting. A common time-waster is the "cobweb caucus" – a long meeting with no focus, covering a broad range of issues in no apparent order.

The "cobweb caucus" can be wiped out by good advance communication. Prepare a written agenda and distribute it to participants ahead of time. This allows everyone to arrive prepared and ensures that the meeting will stay on track. It also helps to invite only those who have a very specific purpose for being there. Too often, people are rounded up just to fill chairs.

Many meetings meander off on irrelevant tangents and get mired in chit chat. To make sure 'fewer fools talk and more wise men speak,' one person should be designated to chair and facilitate the meeting. It's essential that this position be held by a strong communicator – and that means someone who knows when to talk *and* when to listen.

Too often, there is no action plan when a meeting breaks up. What you get is all talk and no results. When a specific objective emerges during a meeting, tasks should be assigned on the spot. And don't forget to follow-up on everyone's assignments, by using your CPs of course. That way you can ensure your objective becomes a reality.

DREAD OF DELEGATION

Many managers seem to live in dread of delegation. A Priority Management survey, *Agenda for the 1990s*, found that in spite of a heavy workload 43 percent of knowledge workers find delegating difficult. And those who do delegate entrust only a small percentage of work to others. Some of us hold the mistaken notion that only we can do the required tasks properly. Others feel that delegation is more trouble than it's worth – that you spend more time explaining than it would take to just do the task yourself.

In the New Knowledge Economy, delegation is essential and unavoidable. It is the key to a productive, interdependent workplace. Effective communication and situational awareness lie at the heart of delegation, and the CP is the perfect tool for delegating.

There are a number of pivotal steps to delegating effectively. First of all, plan before you delegate. Don't delegate what you can simply eliminate – respect the obligations and abilities of others by not wasting their time on trivial items. And don't delay important items by giving priority to more interesting work. If possible, give multiple delegations at once.

Then you should decide who to delegate to. Don't delegate to someone just because they happen to be close at hand, and don't skip levels without checking with a person's supervisor before delegating to them. It's most important to show situational awareness – the person may need more or less coaching depending on their experience with the subject matter. Take their abilities, experience and degree of willingness into account when briefing them.

For a less experienced person, you'll need more follow-up or checkpoints along the way. If a delegation misfires, often it's due to imprecise or poor instructions.

You must then communicate the delegation in writing and tailor it to the individual. Use a CP to back up any oral presentation and avoid the "I didn't know" syndrome. Eliminate any potential confusion over the timing for follow-up activities by setting deadlines, and resolve all priority conflicts over the deadline date ahead of time. Try to hand over the delegation in person whenever possible.

Once you've assigned the task and have established controls and checkpoints, leave the delegatee to get on with it. Don't interfere while the job is in progress – exercise trust. Delegation means passing on authority, not just responsibility.

Finally, reward successful completion of all assigned work. Praise is often the most effective award. Use a mini-CP to say "thank you". For assignments that are unsuccessful or just partially successful, remember to identify errors and shape a positive approach for the future. Always praise in public and correct in private.

It's crucial to resist having the jobs delegated back to you, or you'll end up like a zookeeper. A delegatee may come back to you and say, "I can't seem to do anything with this." What many managers typically say, instead of encouraging them to work out a solution and then return, is, "Just leave it with me." There, you've got one monkey. If you continue to do that, you'll soon have all the monkeys on your back and by noon you'll be running a zoo.

A Priority Manager is a clear and effective communicator – someone who can make meetings, telephone conversations and delegations as productive as possible. With 20/20 memory, your Odyssey to becoming a Priority Manager is almost over. Home is on the horizon.

WHAT IS YOUR INTERDEPENDENCE QUOTIENT?

Strong communication skills are a must in an interdependent workplace. To survive in this environment, you need both communication skills and the ability to cope with change. The move towards interdependence, with the emphasis on teamwork, is more than a passing fad. Are you prepared? Take this quiz to determine your I.Q. (Interdependence Quotient).

1) Do you have experience working in teams? ___ Yes ___No

2) Do you think you are more productive working in teams than working alone? ___ Yes ___No

3) Are you comfortable in a constantly changing environment? ___ Yes ___No

4) Do you cope well working with ambiguity? ___ Yes ___No

5) Do you have a good sense of the direction or mission of the teams you work in? ___ Yes ___No

6) Are you confident in your ability to communicate ideas to a group? ___ Yes ___No

7) Do you consider yourself equally able to lead and follow? ___ Yes ___No

8) Are you comfortable taking risks?   __ Yes __No

9) Do you easily share recognition with others, even if the success

    was due to you?   __ Yes __No

10) Do you use certain techniques to unleash your creativity?   __ Yes __No

HOW DO YOU RATE?

Give yourself two points for each Yes answer and one point for each No.

10-14 points: Look out! You run the risk of not being able to escape the rigidity of the old hierarchical corporate structure. You may not be convinced that interdependence and teamwork are worth the bother. Take another look at what's happening in the world and take steps to develop the skills you need to succeed in an interdependent environment.

15-17 points: You're on your way! You have some of the skills and attitudes needed to be a strong team member, and you don't fear changing conditions. Continue to work on these skills, especially your communication skills.

18-20 points: You have a high I.Q.! If interdependence is the name of the game, you're ready and in fighting form. While change may not come naturally to you, you've learned not to resist it. Your personal confidence is a valuable asset.

THE STRESS FACTOR

O, how full of briers is this working-day world!

WILLIAM SHAKESPEARE, AS YOU LIKE IT

Tina Hoffer, a Banking Industry

manager in Sydney, Australia, was so overstressed a few years ago that she could actually see it when she looked in the mirror – it was written all over her face. She was working 12 to 16 hour days, seven days a week and undertook no activities outside of work. She didn't do anything to help her stress level because she felt she didn't have the time – no time to exercise, read a book for pleasure or shop for clothes and food. She regularly skipped lunch and ordered in at night.

But it took the failure of her marriage to make Tina Hoffer face the fact that her life was out of control. "My marriage was falling apart and I was the last to know," she recalls. "I was so stressed, I didn't know that it had happened."

Although the consequences for Tina Hoffer were extreme, parts of her story may sound very familiar to you. Knowledge workers are all affected day-to-day by some degree of stress. Priority Management's *Agenda for the 1990s* survey found that 81 percent of knowledge workers suffer stress at least once a week, while a startling 48 percent experience some stress every day.

In its earliest manifestation, stress was caused by a threat to our physical well-being – wild animals, hostile tribes, severe weather conditions. In the Information Age, we're not faced with such threats on a daily basis. Stress today is caused by other factors – the perception of too much work, too little time, too few results; ongoing pressure to give of ourselves at home and at work; no time for exercise, reflection and fun.

Stress is now recognized as a major problem facing the business community, as the effects of stress are readily seen in the workplace. In the United States, stress-related illnesses cost hundreds of billions of dollars annually. The signs of stress include headaches, stomach problems, fatigue, muscular tension and nervous irritability. Medical studies indicate that prolonged stress may be a major factor in the development of serious physical illnesses such as heart disease and cancer.

Workplace stress finds its way into the home. It's manifested most commonly through headaches and anger. Other responses vary from procrastination and smoking or overeating, to yelling at children and picking fights with a friend.

One of the reasons stress has become not only a more frequently occurring problem, but also of longer duration, is that we don't allow ourselves "recovery" or "bounce-back" time. Decision-making has become so rapid today, that we don't all have time to decompress and recharge.

By this point in your Odyssey to becoming a Priority Manager, you've acquired the skills to confront stress head-on – and you'll discover that Priority Managers know both how to avoid stress and how to make stress work for them.

AN OUNCE OF PREVENTION

In our attempts to cope with stress, we too often concentrate on a reactive response instead of a proactive approach. We tend to focus on attempts to deal with stress after it has already occurred, rather than dealing with the fundamental causes.

A Priority Manager practices stress avoidance, rather than seeking cures. Priority planning is the best way to keep chronic stress from becoming a lifelong companion. This isn't an aspirin cure, like meditation, deep breathing or relaxation exercises, but a practical technique to arm you against stress.

If you're practicing priority planning by designating your daily activities as 'As' or 'Bs' and setting realistic time estimates for those activities, you're already avoiding a major cause of stress – attempting too much. Successful managers know that in order to complete complex and difficult projects it's important to leave time in their schedules for the unanticipated problems and interruptions that inevitably arise.

In addition to priority planning, make sure you set reasonable deadlines for yourself and that others respect these. Be honest with people about timeframes. And learn how to say a polite, but firm "No" for those times when you've been interrupted once too often, or when someone tries to give you the assignment that could break the camel's back.

If you're continually stressed because you don't have enough time to do things you should and want to do, try reviewing the ways of dealing with time wasters we examined in Chapters 2 and 5. Large amounts of time can be freed up, for example, by learning to delegate, conducting meetings effectively and knowing how to control interruptions. Using your personal organizer should reduce mind traffic, which is a major contributor to stress. As Scott Harris, the busy marketing agency owner and father, said, "If it's not in *The Priority Manager*, it doesn't count."

And if you haven't used the 4-D approach to clearing off your desk yet, do it as soon as possible. Picture your desk as a factory – you can say that you're processing information, that's your raw material. In a factory, the raw materials are never left lying all over the place for people to trip over. Someone could end up breaking their leg and suing. The mess on your desk is more insidious – you're tripping over unfinished work all day long. And rather than breaking a leg, it can break your mind. Such are the effects of "deskstress".

Stress is not necessarily caused by a heavy workload, but by the way you approach your work – how you plan and manage that prickly brier patch we call the working-day world. Yet many people are so caught up in the demands of their work that they can't see beyond it. That's what happened to Tina Hoffer. A Priority Manager knows how to develop a more flexible lifestyle in order to become a more happy, relaxed and effective human being.

Priority Managers lead balanced lives, ones in which their home and work persona are in synch. An effective way to avoid stress is to make sure you're addressing all six important areas of your life – work, learning, physical, social, family and spiritual.

For cumulative stress avoidance, try to choose one activity from any of the areas (except for financial/work) to a total of three every single day. Pursuing challenging and meaningful goals in areas of your life other than work will help you achieve balance and lower stress levels. Here are some examples.

- Learning – take up an instrument, read a book, take a course, learn a new language.

- Physical – exercise regularly; join a sports club; organize a baseball team; learn a new and challenging sport like wind surfing or sport kiting, which is meditative as well as physical.

- Social – give a theme dinner party; join a volunteer group, choir or service organization.

- Family – do crafts with your children; build a tree house; plan a short, romantic get-away with your partner, arrange a family get-together, write letters.

- Spiritual – take time for reflection during long walks in parks and along riversides; attend a service at the church, temple or synagogue of your choice.

While you're at it, resist the temptation to become a playaholic. Overscheduling your leisure time can be just as stressful as having no leisure time at all.

Ever since Tina Hoffer became a Priority Manager three years ago and recognized the value of a balanced lifestyle, her life has turned around. She has reduced her working day by at least four hours. She's remarried, bought a house and people have been commenting on her change in personality – a change for the better. She's even taken to participating in triathlons, just for fun.

Her workload hasn't changed, but how she manages it all has. Priority planning has helped Tina Hoffer become more focussed and she has learned how to handle interruptions and to delegate, something she wasn't willing to do before. Using her personal organizer has also significantly reduced her stress level. "Now it's not stress in the mind," she says, "It's stress on paper. I've dumped everything into *The Priority Manager*, and I know it's going to get it done."

If you asked Tina to name one of the changes she's most proud of, she'd probably tell you, "I now remember people's birthdays."

STRESS AND SUCCESS

Earlier generations may have suffered from just as much stress, but now we're talking about it more. Maybe life in this complex, highly urbanized and ever-changing society is in fact more stressful than it was in the past. At times we seem almost obsessed with stress – comparing our stress levels over at the water cooler as ancient warriors may have compared battle scars. Even children as young as six talk of being stressed. They've either overheard their parents incessantly talking about it, or they genuinely feel stress due to the overscheduling of their lives by anxious – and stressed – parents.

You might dream of a stress-free life, but in fact we need some stress to keep us motivated and productive. Not all stress is bad—it's only when we aren't able to manage it that stress becomes distress. Interestingly enough, despite the statistics that indicate we're working harder and spending less time on leisure, hard work itself doesn't necessarily create stress. In fact, a survey of top executives throughout North America shows that they thrive on stress. They work hard and enjoy it.

Stress can't be attributed to work alone. It's also a consequence of the kind of person you are, the circumstances you find yourself in and the way you handle demands placed upon you. Balancing your life, priority planning, learning to delegate and to say "No," are all ways to avoid or reduce stress. But what about those pressure-cooker situations when stress is unavoidable?

Consider the life of a world-class athlete. Few of us are asked to perform under the same pressure and stress as those who compete at the very highest levels in sports. An Olympic runner, for example, has only one chance in four years to go for the gold – maybe one chance in a lifetime. An entire lifetime of hard work and training must pay off in only a few minutes, or even mere seconds, of peak performance. Now that's stress.

Yet the great majority of world-class athletes don't collapse under pressure, but channel their stress into a highly-focussed energy that propels them towards their personal best performance. As a Priority Manager, you too can take advantage of those extremely stressful situations that do arise by allowing the pressure to propel you forward instead of paralyzing you.

Now that you're a stress manager, your Odyssey is almost over.

CHOICE, NOT CHANCE

*We should all be concerned about the future,
because we will have to spend the rest of our lives there.*

CHARLES KETTERING, 1876-1958

A BUSINESSMAN WHO FREQUENTLY

travels makes it a point to ask a flight attendant for a comment card shortly before take-off. Invariably, the flight attendant shows great concern at his request and asks,"Is anything wrong, sir?" "No," he always replies, smiling. Then he adds, firmly, "But I would like a comment card, please."

For the remainder of the flight, he tends to receive impeccable service – no matter which airline he's on, no matter who the attendant is.

This businessman has a firm handle on "proactive futuring". He is actively making the future he envisions happen – doing something now in order to get positive results later. What would he achieve if he waited until service was lousy and then complained? Inadequate service, an apology and uncomfortable feelings all around. Instead, he settles into his seat and launches a pre-emptive strike.

Priority Managers know that the future they desire will only happen if they go after it themselves. The best way to predict the future is to invent it for yourself. No one else is going to make things happen for you. Now that you've successfully reached the end of your Odyssey and are a Priority Manager, you know that only through personal strategic planning can you become proactive about your future. Bring the future into the present today – through choice, not chance.

In an environment of constant flux, you need focus as well as flexibility. By determining short and long-term goals, you can move towards a future vision while negotiating the difficult terrain of today's business and personal worlds. Learning cannot stop once you've arrived "home." With so many changes altering your everyday world, you must continue to learn throughout your career.

A firm foundation of essential management skills and a commitment to lifelong learning will guarantee you land surefootedly in the 21st century. Control of the present means you can now cast your mind forward and unlock the power of your potential. The future begins today.

WORKING SMARTER - LIVING SMARTER

The challenge of the future is not to work *harder*, but to work and live *smarter*. Working smarter means reviewing your company's values on a regular basis and aligning them with your personal values. This will help you avoid slipping back into the values gap. Living smarter means making your values clear to your family and friends, understanding theirs and setting priorities for the ones that are most important to you.

Working and living smarter also means being a Priority Manager all 86,400 seconds of the day. The pace of life and the rapid flow of information don't appear to be slowing down, so the continual use of the skills you've acquired as a Priority Manager is essential.

Managing interruptions, conscious decision-making, prioritizing activities, effective communication and delegation, avoiding stress, and aiming for balance are all essential skills of a Priority Manager. But the most critical skill of all is the ability, and willingness, to plan.

Control starts with planning. You need a plan for your life, your month, your week and your day. As you now know, all knowledge work begins with output, and that relates not only to work, but to your home and personal life as well. That means all your activities should be future-oriented in the sense that everything you do leads to a goal, no matter how small.

That goal might be simply to get home by 6 p.m. every day, bring a small project in under budget or make a pancake breakfast on Sunday for the entire family. And it might be as large as wanting to be marketing vice-president in two years, moving to your dream city of Phoenix, Montreal, or London, or completing a competitive triathlon. But the goal must exist before you can even take one tiny step towards it.

Imagine if you're in a strange city leaving point 'A' and trying to get to point 'B', but you continually have road blocks and detours thrown in your way. You might have had some idea of how to get to where you wanted to go when you started out, but after the third detour you're totally lost. Where would you be without a roadmap? Yet that's what many knowledge workers do — keep themselves frantically busy dealing with the detours until it dawns on them that they don't even know to what end.

Or think of it this way: you're shooting arrows into the side of an old barn. Do you draw the target before or after you've pulled back the bow?

A Priority Management survey, *The 21st Century Workplace*, found that of those people who say they're happy with life in general, most have a plan to achieve their goals. Planning beyond the short term is vital. Priority Management's *IMS Report* shows that following training, 72 percent of the respondents said they had written a three-year strategic plan.

Planning begins at the daily level and then for some businesspeople moves right up to five years, or even longer. You can get into the planning habit by giving yourself a 10 minute planning workout in your *Priority Manager* at the end of every workday. It's important that you plan for the following day *before* leaving the office. That way you eliminate mind traffic for the rest of the afternoon and evening, relate better to your spouse and children, sleep more soundly and wake up to a purpose – not just an alarm.

The first step in the workout is to check the calendar for the next day's appointments and meetings, and transfer these to the Plan page. Allow for travelling time, and include personal and social commitments, too. Then pencil in time on the Plan page for sleep and other routine activities. The third step is to assign priorities to the items on the Activities page and schedule time on the Plan page for the 'A' activities. And finally, schedule time for the 'B' activities.

You should also take a couple of minutes just before going to bed to record your achievements. By reviewing the six important areas of life on the balance wheel, you'll become aware of where you may be short-changing yourself or those around you. If you've set goals for yourself in all six areas, the activities you undertake should have an incremental effect. That way you will move closer to your goals every day, closer to the future you envision for yourself.

The definition of personal success continues to evolve in the 1990s. There is a growing awareness that success is not confined to the office, but is a by-product of every aspect of life. In the 1990s and beyond, the challenge will be to make sure the six areas of your life – work, learning, physical, social, family and spiritual – have struck a meaningful balance.

At the end of any day, a Priority Manager should be able to close his or her eyes to take the Tombstone Test and be more than content with the outcome. It's a satisfying thing to know that you can control your own legacy. In *A Psalm of Life*, Henry Wadsworth Longfellow wrote:

Lives of great men all remind us
We can make our lives sublime,
And, departing, leave behind us
Footprints on the sands of time.

THE EFFECTIVENESS CHALLENGE

Happy he who like Ulysses
a glorious voyage made.

JOACHIM DU BELLAY, 1522-1560

WELCOME HOME! THE ROAD TO BECOMING

a Priority Manager is not always smooth, but no worthwhile Odyssey is without its obstacles. I hope you are starting to enjoy the rewards of coming "home". Sometimes we need to be reminded just who and what are important in life.

Since developing the Priority Management system, I have been gratified to hear from thousands of people across North America, Europe, Australia, New Zealand and the Far East who are startled and delighted by the results of priority planning. The biggest reward they report is finding a way to be more involved with their family *and* increase their effectiveness at work. I know what a joy that can be.

As we move towards the 21st century, we are taking on new challenges. Working smarter means more than simply being organized; on a larger scale it means increasing white collar productivity. Investment in technology has outpaced white collar productivity in recent years. Studies show that the cost of running an office increases each year, but that extra cost is not met by higher productivity.

Productivity is a factor of both work tools and work processes. This book has addressed *The Priority Manager* as a tool. The next step is to improve the processes of knowledge work.

With the knowledge worker revolution just about complete, we face a new challenge – how to measure productivity and quality in knowledge jobs. In order to increase effectiveness, it must first be measured. Quite simply, if you can't measure it, you can't manage it. In blue collar work, productivity measurement is relatively straightforward – divide output by labor, machinery and other costs. But for a marketing manager, for example, what do we measure? And how?

The raw material of the knowledge worker is information, and like all work, knowledge work is comprised of three dimensions or phases – deciding, doing and delivering. For instance, a photocopier saleperson will 'decide' who to target and how to make the sale presentation. 'Doing' lies in researching and preparing the presentation. And 'delivery' involves making and closing the sale, as well as follow-up service. This '3D' formula can be applied to any knowledge job. The answer to measuring and improving white-collar productivity lies in identifying the key processes of knowledge work and assessing the competence of individuals in each of these three areas.

Following years of research and study, Priority Management has developed a tool for measuring white collar productivity. The Process-Skills Analysis is an instrument uniquely placed to establish effectiveness benchmarks for knowledge and service workers. It is based on a thorough analysis of the eight key processes which form the foundation of all knowledge work. When performed effectively, these eight key processes combine to enhance the productivity (P), quality (Q) and interdependence (I) – the PQ-I – of knowledge workers, regardless of their function or seniority.

The Process-Skills Analysis feedback report presents a graphic summary of scores obtained for the eight processes, a narrative description and interpretation of each process score, an effectiveness gap analysis and guidance on the preparation of a PQ-I Development Plan.

Through the Process-Skills Analysis, you can determine the effectiveness of individuals, teams and entire organizations, while also providing insight into how you measure up to the effectiveness challenge of the 1990s and 21st century.

By becoming a Priority Manager you have acquired the right tools to be an effective knowledge worker. Now you can take the next step towards increasing your productivity and effectiveness through the Process-Skills Analysis.

In the meantime, I hope you are already reaping the benefits of your Priority Management training. You will continue to encounter obstacles such as the Time Crunch, stress and the challenge of coping with constant change. The difference being that you are now equipped with a tool that will help you remain in control of your life. The *Priority Manager* enables you to enjoy higher productivity at work, gain more time for the other important things in your life and reduce stress levels in the bargain. Most exciting of all, your life today and in the future will be determined by choice, not chance.

If your Odyssey to become a Priority Manager has helped you rediscover important values, given you a second chance to be a better parent or spouse, aided in achieving a goal at work or simply helped you put more fun in your life, I will be more than content with my own Tombstone Test.

Daniel Stamp

ACKNOWLEDGEMENT

I wish to acknowledge the support, encouragement and many contributions of my fellow adventurers, my team of interdependent businesspeople – the Priority Management Associates. Risk-takers all, these vanguards of the New Knowledge Economy embrace change in their own lives and have come to embody the spirit of the Priority Manager. It is not difficult to see how they have, in turn, inspired countless individuals around the world to reach the power of their potential and helped create the #1 management training company in the world. My thanks to one and all.

Special thanks go to those who helped turn my intentions into actions, by making this book a reality. To Karen Speirs and Zsuzsi Gartner for their assistance with the manuscript, to Russ Willms and Suburbia Studios for the creative artwork and especially to my colleagues in Vancouver, Seattle and our corporate offices worldwide who have kept the ship afloat while I've been away from the helm.

Finally, I would like to thank my wife, Georgina, for her editing talents, helpful insights and unwavering support, and my children – Rebekah, Elizabeth, Joanna and Jonathan – for their love and patience throughout this particular Odyssey.

PRIORITY
MANAGEMENT®

HELPING PEOPLE TURN INTENTIONS INTO ACTIONS. WORLDWIDE.

Australia	Belgium	France	Hong Kong	Italy	New Zealand	Portugal
Rep. of Ireland	Singapore	Spain	Puerto Rico	Taiwan	The Netherlands	United Kingdom

INTERNATIONAL HEADQUARTERS:
IBM Tower, P.O. Box 10105, 1700-701 West Georgia Street, Vancouver, B.C., Canada V7Y 1C6 1-800-665-5448
UNITED STATES HEADQUARTERS:
Koll Center Bellevue, 500-108th Avenue N.E., Suite 1740, Bellevue, WA, USA 98004 1-800-221-9031

NOTES

NOTES